1 9 8 2

The Year
I Was Born

Compiled by Sally Tagholm

Illustrated by Michael Evans

FANTAIL

in association with Signpost Books

FANTAIL PUBLISHING, AN IMPRINT OF PUFFIN ENTERPRISES
Published by the Penguin Group
27 Wrights Lane London W8 5TZ, England
Viking Penguin Inc., 40 West 23rd Street, New York, NY 10010, USA
Penguin Books Australia, Ltd., Ringwood, Victoria, Australia
Penguin Books Canada, Ltd., 2801 John Street, Markham, Ontario,
Canada L3R 1B4
Penguin Books Ltd., Registered Offices: Harmondsworth, Middlesex,
England
Published by Penguin Books in association with Signpost Books

First published 1990
10 9 8 7 6 5 4 3 2 1

Based on an original idea by Sally Wood
Conceived, designed and produced by Signpost Books Ltd, 1989
Copyright in this format © 1990 Signpost Books Ltd.,
44 Uxbridge Street London W8 7TG
England

Illustrations copyright © 1990 Michael Evans
Text copyright © 1990 Sally Tagholm
Pasteup: Naomi Games
Editor: Dorothy Wood

ISBN 0140 90200 7

All rights reserved

Colour separations by Fotographics, Ltd.
Printed and bound in Belgium by Proost Book Production through
Landmark Production Consultants, Ltd.

Typeset by AKM Associates (UK) Ltd, Ajmal House, Hayes Road,
Southall, London

ME

Name: RUSSELL DAVID HARRISON

Date of birth: 11-2-82

Time of birth: 2-05 AM

Place of birth: SHRODELLS (WATFORD GENERAL)

Weight at birth:

Colour of eyes: BLUE

Colour of hair (if any): VERY DARK

Distinguishing marks:

Mum

Dad

Sister/Brother

Sister/Brother

MY FAMILY

January

Friday
January 1

Operation Sea Fire launches Maritime England Year with coastal beacons all the way round England.

Saturday
January 2

Erica Roe takes off her top and runs across the pitch at Twickenham during a Rugby International between England and Australia.

Sunday
January 3

Hundreds of sea birds, covered in thick black oil, are washed up on the coast of East Anglia.

Monday
January 4

Melting snow! Heavy rain! Floods! The High Street in Boroughbridge, north Yorkshire, is under 1.2m of water.

Tuesday
January 5

A Lakeland terrier is rescued after spending 28hrs stuck in a rabbit warren at Chilwell in Nottinghamshire.

Wednesday
January 6

The QE2 is stuck on a mudbank for 2hrs in San Juan harbour, in Puerto Rico, with 2000 passengers on board.

Thursday
January 7

The floods freeze in York and icebergs are reported floating down the street!

Friday
January 8

Worst blizzards in living memory! Birmingham and Gatwick airports are closed; cauliflowers in Lincolnshire and Kent are wiped out.

Saturday
January 9

Scotland is colder than the South Pole!
All roads in Wales are closed.

Full Moon

Sunday
January 10

It is –26.1°C at Newport in Shropshire—the lowest temperature ever recorded in England!
It is –27.2°C at Braemar in Scotland, which equals the lowest temperature ever recorded in Britain!

Monday
January 11

Dr Who's Tardis appears at Heathrow airport in London, and Mrs Thatcher's son, Mark, disappears in the Sahara Desert during a car rally.

Tuesday
January 12

A chimp called Benjie is born at Regent's Park Zoo in London.

Wednesday
January 13

Happy Birthday Michael Bond, creator of Paddington Bear! Severe shortage of wellington boots is reported throughout the country.

Thursday
January 14

Mark Thatcher is rescued from the Sahara Desert, after being spotted by a search plane.

January

Named after the Roman god, Janus, who had two faces and could look backwards and forwards at the same time. Also known as 'frosty-month', 'wolf-month', 'after-yule', 'first-month' and 'snow-month'.

Year of the Dog

January 25 1982 – February 12 1983

Chinese horoscopes have nothing to do with western signs of the zodiac. They follow a 12 year cycle, with each year represented by an animal. According to legend, the Buddha summoned all the animals in the world to him one New Year, promising them a reward. Only twelve obeyed and he gave each of a them a year, with the one who arrived first getting the first year! The order is always the same: the Rat, the Buffalo, the Tiger, the Cat, the Dragon, the Snake, the Horse, the Goat, the Monkey, the Cockerel, the Dog and the Pig.

The Chinese year is based on the moon and not the sun. There are 12 new moons in each year, with a 13th added every 12 years. This means that New Year never falls on the same day!

Typical Dogs are always on their guard, alert and watching! They don't show their feelings very often—only when strictly necessary. However, they are always the first to speak out against injustice. Although Dogs are great worriers, they are loyal, faithful, honest and have a deep sense of duty, inspiring the highest confidence in others! The Dog can be happy with the Horse, makes a good team with the Tiger but will find peace and quiet with the Cat. Famous Dogs include Socrates, Louis XVI, Lenin and Yuri Gagarin!

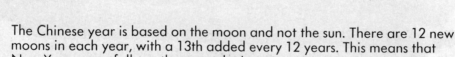

DAILY MOON (15p)

SEVEN PEOPLE MAROONED IN TRAIN BY SNOW RESCUED BY HELICOPTER

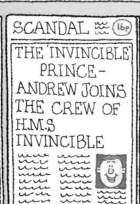

SCANDAL (16p)

THE 'INVINCIBLE' PRINCE—ANDREW JOINS THE CREW OF H.M.S INVINCIBLE

THE DAILY OWL 14p

PLANE CRASH IN WASHINGTON. BOEING 737 PLUNGES INTO BRIDGE AT RUSH HOUR

BLAG 16p

NO TRAINS—RAIL STRIKE CONTINUES.

Friday *January 15*	Tracy Dodds, from the Wirral, is crowned Miss Great Britain.
Saturday *January 16*	Three British entrants leave the Grantham Webb Hotel, nr Dover, at the start of the Monte Carlo Rally.
Sunday *January 17*	Members of the British Sub-Aqua Club's Holborn branch spend 1hr 15mins in the Serpentine in Hyde Park, London, to raise money for charity.
Monday *January 18*	A(lan) A(lexander) Milne was born 100 years ago today.
Tuesday *January 19*	The new Billingsgate Fish Market at West India Dock, Tower Hamlets in London, opens at 5.30am.
Wednesday *January 20*	Ocenebra Erinaca (snails) are stealing the oysters from the beds in the Solent! They drill holes in the oysters' shell and eat the contents.
Thursday *January 21*	Land's End has been sold for £1,750,000.
Friday *January 22*	Children in Dymchurch, Kent, beat the rail strike by taking the miniature railway to school in New Romney.
Saturday *January 23*	Princess Diana goes to a school fair in Brixton, London, and buys a tin of baked beans (10p) and a mango (£1.50)
Sunday *January 24*	Chris Wreghitt (23) wins the National Cyclo-Cross Championship in Birmingham for the fifth time in a row.
Monday *January 25*	A reception at the House of Commons launches the Year of the Scout. Guests include famous ex-Scouts Sir Harold Wilson, Frankie Howerd and David Bellamy. New Moon Beginning of the Chinese YEAR OF THE DOG!
Tuesday *January 26*	Margaret Cross (19) from Brownlow High School in County Armagh, wins the Top School Cook Competition with Coquilles de Cabillaud (cod poached in lemon juice, with a sauce of mushrooms, cheese and mace).
Wednesday *January 27*	Disc jockey, Dave Lee Travis, is named Pipeman of the Year.
Thursday *January 28*	PG Tips chimps, Louis and Jill, give a party at the Waldorf Hotel in London to celebrate the TV commercial's twenty-fifth birthday.

Friday *January 29*	Almost all the young coypus (large rodents, which escaped into the wild from fur farms in the 1930s) in East Anglia have been wiped out by the cold weather.
Saturday *January 30*	Fortieth anniversary edition of 'Desert Island Discs': the castaway is Paul McCartney.
Sunday *January 31*	The World Ski Championships continue in Austria despite torrential rain—thanks to Ski Cement, which is spread on the pistes!

Operation Sea Fire
organised by Bruno Peek

The Earl Nelson of Trafalgar lights the first beacon at Great Yarmouth at midnight on January 1st. The ring of beacons then goes right round England. Each one is lit when the one before it becomes visible.

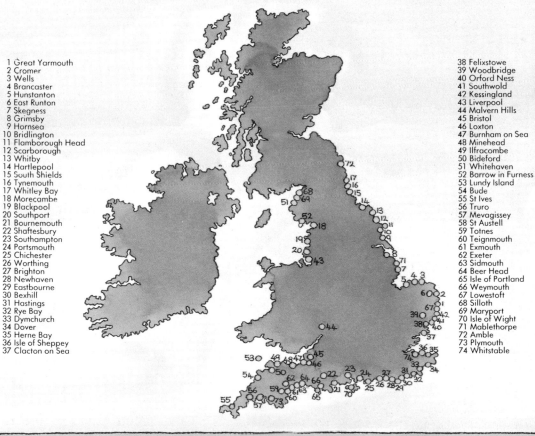

1 Great Yarmouth
2 Cromer
3 Wells
4 Brancaster
5 Hunstanton
6 East Runton
7 Skegness
8 Grimsby
9 Hornsea
10 Bridlington
11 Flamborough Head
12 Scarborough
13 Whitby
14 Hartlepool
15 South Shields
16 Tynemouth
17 Whitley Bay
18 Morecambe
19 Blackpool
20 Southport
21 Bournemouth
22 Shaftesbury
23 Southampton
24 Portsmouth
25 Chichester
26 Worthing
27 Brighton
28 Newhaven
29 Eastbourne
30 Bexhill
31 Hastings
32 Rye Bay
33 Dymchurch
34 Dover
35 Herne Bay
36 Isle of Sheppey
37 Clacton on Sea

38 Felixstowe
39 Woodbridge
40 Orford Ness
41 Southwold
42 Kessingland
43 Liverpool
44 Malvern Hills
45 Bristol
46 Loxton
47 Burnham on Sea
48 Minehead
49 Ilfracombe
50 Bideford
51 Whitehaven
52 Barrow in Furness
53 Lundy Island
54 Bude
55 St Ives
56 Truro
57 Mevagissey
58 St Austell
59 Totnes
60 Teignmouth
61 Exmouth
62 Exeter
63 Sidmouth
64 Beer Head
65 Isle of Portland
66 Weymouth
67 Lowestoft
68 Silloth
69 Maryport
70 Isle of Wight
71 Mablethorpe
72 Amble
73 Plymouth
74 Whitstable

February

Monday *February 1*	Postal charges go up by 9.3%. The new rates are 15½p for a first class and 12½p for a second class letter.
Tuesday *February 2*	The Roman Catholic Church approves the official souvenirs for the Pope's visit to Britain. They all carry the special emblem—a cross inset with papal keys.
Wednesday *February 3*	The Princess of Wales agrees to becomes patron or president of the Royal School for the Blind, the Welsh National Opera, the Malcolm Sargent Cancer Fund for Children.
Thursday *February 4*	For Sale: the Royal Navy's only hydrofoil—the 117-tonne *HMS Speedy*.
Friday *February 5*	Laker Airways collapses, owing £270,000,000, and leaving 6,000 passengers stranded around the world. Rain!
Saturday *February 6*	Thirtieth anniversary of the Queen's accession to the throne. Happy Birthday President Reagan—71 today!
Sunday *February 7*	Sir Ranulph Fiennes and Charles Burton, of the Transglobe Expedition, postpone their attempt to cross the North Pole. Sir Ranulph has a cracked tooth, and is flown to the dentist instead!
Monday *February 8*	David Springbett flies from Blackfriars in London to Wall Street in New York in helicopters and on Concorde in 3hrs 59mins 44secs! He beats the previous record set in 1979 by 10mins 59secs. Full Moon
Tuesday *February 9*	Centenary of the British Veterinary Association in London.
Wednesday *February 10*	The Royal Mint unveils the new £1 and 20p coins, which become legal tender today. The 20p will go into circulation in June and the £1 next year.
Thursday *February 11*	Red rain falls over parts of southern England. It's fine dust blown from the Sahara Desert.
Friday *February 12*	Opening of the eighty-sixth Crufts Dog Show at Earl's Court in London. Entries total 9844 dogs and for the first time it lasts for three days.
Saturday *February 13*	The members of the Transglobe Expedition set off from base camp across the Arctic to the North Pole. With them goes Bothie, a Jack Russell terrier!

Sunday *February 14*	Valentine's Day! Grayco Hazelnut(3) is named Supreme Champion at Crufts—the first toy poodle to win the title since 1966.
Monday *February 15*	The 1319-tonne *Dunedin* left New Zealand for England 100 years ago today with the first cargo of refrigerated lamb. A modern container ship is retracing the voyage.
Tuesday *February 16*	In Egypt British archeologists have discovered the 3300-year-old tomb of Princess Tia, daughter of King Seti I and Queen Tui, and sister of Ramases II.

February

The Roman month of purification. The name comes from the Latin 'februo' which means 'I purify by sacrifice'. It has also been known as 'sprout kale' and 'rain month'.

10 Feb: new stamps to mark the centenary of Charles Darwin.

Hearing Dogs for the Deaf

Launched at Crufts in 1982, Hearing Dogs are trained to recognize and respond to different sounds so that they can alert their deaf owners by touching them and leading them to the source of the sound. The dogs that are used are either strays that have been rescued, or unwanted dogs. They have to be friendly, out-going, alert and inquisitive: terrier-type mongrels are often best, although both Chihuahuas and Old English Sheepdogs have been used!

The First British Hearing Dog 'Favour', an 8-month-old mongrel, was rescued by the National Canine Defence League, and made his first appearance at Crufts in 1982.

Some sounds that Hearing Dogs are trained to recognize:
Doorbell
Alarm clock
Smoke alarm
Baby's cry
Cooker timer
Telephone
Kettle boiling

SNOOP ~~~~~17P
POLICE DOGS GET PROTECTIVE CLOTHING

DAILY BEACON
~~~15P
THE POUND IN YOUR POCKET IS NOW A COIN

THE SCRIBBLE 14P
AMERICA, SAUDI ARABIA AND JAPAN ALL WANT THE SS.80-THE ELECTRONIC SCARECROW

EAVESDROPPER
18P ~~~~~
LAKER AIRWAYS THE PIONEER OF THE CHEAP TRANS-ATLANTIC FLIGHT GOES BUST

Wednesday February 17	Snow in the south and west! Worst hit are Salisbury Plain, the Cotswolds and the Chilterns. It is –9°C at Glenlivet in the Cairngorms.
Thursday February 18	The 6-week-long train drivers' dispute is called off.
Friday February 19	Angry French wine growers seize an Italian tanker on the motorway near Montpellier and empty 39,996 litres of Italian red wine onto the carriageway!
Saturday February 20	A cat's eye stud that warns motorists of black ice is being developed at Nottingham University. When the temperature drops below freezing, it turns blue!
Sunday February 21	A polar bear called Twinkle arrives at Chester Zoo. She is 7 years old, weighs 227kg and comes from Toronto Zoo, Canada.
Monday February 22	Three pink flamingoes, 2 buff turkeys, 1 damozel crane and 1 Muscovy duck have been ravaged in the past week by a fox at the exotic bird compound in Holland Park, London. The survivors have been moved to Crystal Palace children's zoo.
Tuesday February 23	Pancake Day! Mrs Rosemary Ludgate wins the annual Pancake Day Race at Olney in Buckinghamshire for the third time running—379.3 metres in 1min 5.5secs! New Moon
Wednesday February 24	Major General Michael Walsh succeeds Sir William Gladstone as Chief Scout.
Thursday February 25	The Queen attends the opening of the annual Trial of the Pyx at Goldsmiths' Hall, London. A jury of Freemen of the Goldsmiths' Company tests coins from the Royal Mint to make sure they are perfect.
Friday February 26	£2,250 has been granted to the Norfolk Pillar in Great Yarmouth. It was built in 1818 as a monument to Lord Nelson—20 years before the one in Trafalgar Square!
Saturday February 27	Made-to-measure body armour for police dogs is being developed: it protects the dog's neck, back, sides and chest.
Sunday February 28	The SS80 electronic scarecrow, invented by Michael Williams of Essex, is 2.4m high, waves its arms in the air and moans through a powerful air horn.

March

Monday *March 1*	St David's Day. The unmanned Soviet space module, Venera 13, lands on Venus, after a 4 month flight and 300,000,000km!
Tuesday *March 2*	The Duke of Edinburgh visits the Dehiwela Zoological Gardens, near Colombo, in Sri Lanka, and is given a 2-year-old baby elephant from the elephant orphanage.
Wednesday *March 3*	Hurricane Isaac destroys the entire yam crop on the island of Tonga in the south Pacific.
Thursday *March 4*	The RSPB has bought 36.45 hectares of the Loons, a marshland on the north-west mainland of Orkney. Inhabitants include species of breeding ducks.
Friday *March 5*	Sir Ranulph Fiennes and Charles Burton are about 724km from the North Pole now. The temperature is –40°C!
Saturday *March 6*	Twenty thousand people visit the new Barbican Centre in London today, after its official opening on March 3.
Sunday *March 7*	The annual cull of harp seal pups in Canada starts today—nearly a week late because of bad weather. Protestors plan to use hovercraft to disrupt the slaughter.
Monday *March 8*	Children celebrate Commonwealth Day by releasing 46 balloons at the Commonwealth Institute in London – 1 for each member nation.
Tuesday *March 9*	Budget Day: weekly child benefit goes up by 60p to £5.85 from November. Full Moon
Wednesday *March 10*	Happy Eighteenth Birthday, Prince Edward! He comes of age, but, as a member of the Royal Family, can't vote.
Thursday *March 11*	New regulations announced in China: only one child allowed unless there are very special circumstances.
Friday *March 12*	Bulu, the first orang-utan to be born at London Zoo, celebrates her 21st birthday AND a new grandson, Jago, born today!
Saturday *March 13*	Appearing in London: advertisements on the sides of taxis.
Sunday *March 14*	One of the Transglobe Expedition's skidoos (a kind of snow-mobile) disappears into a crevasse, but two crates of vital supplies are rescued before it vanishes.

Monday *March 15*	Heavy snowfalls in Gloucestershire and Wiltshire and floods in the Thames valley.
Tuesday *March 16*	Hail, thunder and snow over much of England. A new skidoo, a sledge and other equipment are delivered to the Transglobe team by aeroplane.
Wednesday *March 17*	St Patrick's Day. A statue of Sir Winston Churchill outside the British Embassy in Washington is sprayed green.
Thursday *March 18*	Day and night are almost exactly the same length today: the sun rises at 6.9am and sets at 6.10pm.
Friday *March 19*	Mount St Helen's, in Washington State, USA, erupts: a 259 sq. km red danger zone is closed off.
Saturday *March 20*	Spring Equinox: the Sun crosses the celestial equator from south to north.
Sunday *March 21*	Mothering Sunday. Philip Edwards and Mark Brockham make history by coxing the first and second eights in the Women's Boat Race.
Monday *March 22*	The American space shuttle Columbia blasts off, on its third mission, from Cape Canaveral in Florida.
Tuesday *March 23*	Columbia's crew report that 37 of the craft's 30,000 heat shield tiles are missing!
Wednesday *March 24*	There is a 1-in-2,000,000 chance that we might collide with the comet Swift-Tuttle this year. It was first seen in 1862 and is meant to come back from deep space every 120 years!
Thursday *March 25*	A colony of tropical green parakeets is nesting at Northdown Park in Margate: it started when two birds escaped from a pet shop. New Moon
Friday *March 26*	The Timeball Tower at Deal, Kent, which has been out of action for more than 50 years, is to be restored to working order.
Saturday *March 27*	The comic *Eagle* is re-launched after 12 years (price 20p), complete with free Space Spinner, Dan Dare and the Return of the Mekon. It first appeared on April 14, 1950.
Sunday *March 28*	Clocks go forward 1hr when British Summer Time starts at 1am. The Dutch yacht *Flyer* is leading the Round-the-World Yacht Race towards the finishing line at Southsea.

Monday *March 29*	A volcano in Mexico, El Chinchonal, erupts. The Dutch yacht *Flyer* crosses the finishing line at 8.47am, smashing the 43,443km race record by 2 weeks.
Tuesday *March 30*	Columbia touches down after 8 days in orbit and after her scientific instruments record a massive solar flare.
Wednesday *March 31*	The two-hundred-and-fiftieth anniversary of the composer Haydn's birth.

A rainy, sunny month!

March

Named after the Roman god Mars. It has also been known as 'rough-month', 'lengthening month', 'boisterous month' and 'windy month'.

The Soviet space craft Venera 13, and her sister ship which lands on Venus on March 5, send back colour pictures which show that the planet consists largely of basalt rock. Its surface is a combination of huge sand dunes and rocky terrain, the sky is dark orange and the temperature is about 482°C!

New stamps celebrating Youth Organizations – on the 75th anniversary of the Boy Scout Movement and the 125th anniversary of the birth of its founder, Lord Baden-Powell.

15½p · 19½p · 26p · 29p

GASP   15p
TORVILL AND DEAN DO IT AGAIN! THEY RETAIN WORLD ICE DANCE TITLE

LOUD HAILER   12p
TROUBLE BREWS IN THE FALKLAND ISLANDS

DAILY SENSATION
INDIAN P.M. OPENS FESTIVAL OF INDIA IN LONDON

THE COMET   16p
SOON YOU'LL BE ABLE TO GET 60 TV STATIONS. SATELLITE TV GETS GO AHEAD

U.K. Fact File 1982

Total area of the United Kingdom   244,099.7sq km

Capital City   London (157,9.9sq km: population 6,696,000)

Population of UK
55,776,000

Females
28,701,000

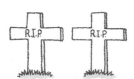

Males
27,064,000

Births

719,200

Marriages
387,000

Deaths   662,800

Most popular boys' name

Most popular girls' name

Licensed vehicles   19,770,000
Driving tests   2,005,300
(51.9% failed)

Telephones   28,400,000

Brownies
419,000
Cubs
302,000

Girl Guides
336,000
Boy Scouts
231,000

Head of State
Queen Elizabeth II

Prime Minister
Margaret Hilda Thatcher

Poet Laureate
Sir John Betjeman

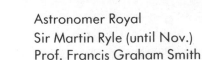

Astronomer Royal
Sir Martin Ryle (until Nov.)
Prof. Francis Graham Smith

April

Thursday *April 1*	Scientists report that the Chinese mung beans grown in space aboard the shuttle Columbia were very confused by the lack of gravity—they twisted and turned in several directions and the roots sprouted out of the soil!
Friday *April 2*	Argentina invades the Falkland Islands in the South Atlantic. The Prince and Princess of Wales open the Pagoda of a Hundred Harmonies in Chinatown in Liverpool.
Saturday *April 3*	The Grand National is won by Grittar, ridden by Dick Saunders. Geraldine Rees becomes the first woman to complete the course – on Cheers!
Sunday *April 4*	A 4-hectare bird sanctuary is opened by the River Neme at Peterborough in Cambridgeshire, where more than 180 species have been spotted over the last 3 years.
Monday *April 5*	Britain's Task Force, led by the carriers *Invincible* and *Hermes*, leave Portsmouth for the Falklands. The Foreign Secretary, Lord Carrington, resigns.
Tuesday *April 6*	Americans Robert Peary and Matthew Henson claim to have reached the North Pole — in 1909. The Transglobe expedition is about 160km away from it now.

Thousands of people are stranded after the Mexican volcano, El Chinchonal, erupts again.

Wednesday *April 7*	Albert Barnes, editor of the comic *Dandy* for 45 years (and the creator of Desperate Dan), is retiring this week.
Thursday *April 8*	The river Thames rises: London is on flood alert! The Queen distributes Maundy money in St David's Cathedral, Dyfed. The 56 men and 56 women who receive it match the Queen's age: she will be 56 on April 21.
Friday *April 9*	Chay Blyth, David Wilkie, Sharon Davis and Steve Ovett raise £50,000 in a swimming marathon towards the cost of lifting the wreck of the *Mary Rose* from the Solent.
Saturday *April 10*	Mount Galunggung, a volcano 169km south east of Jakarta, the capital of Indonesia, erupts for the second time this week.
Sunday *April 11*	Easter Sunday. Sir Ranulph Fiennes, Charles Burton and Bothie reach the North Pole, 31 months after they left Greenwich. They become the first men (and dog) to have been to both North and South Poles.

Monday *April 12*	Bank Holiday. Britain declares a 322km war zone around the Falklands from 4am. Annual elver eating competition at Frampton on Severn, Gloucestershire: Ian Mould (33) eats nearly 500gm of baby eels in 39 secs!
Tuesday *April 13*	The liner, *Uganda*, is requisitioned by the government for the Falklands. The 900 children on board return home after their cruise is cut short.
Wednesday *April 14*	Mrs Peggy Kemp, from Croydon, has won the Chinn Lantern Award in the London Bonsai Competition: one of her entries is a larch tree with both old and new cones on it.
Thursday *April 15*	Unofficial hang gliding record is set by Bob Calvert, who flies from Sarn Hill, Powys, to Hindon near Salisbury Plain—180kms in 4hrs. 20mins. He flew as high as 1,829m and his eyebrows froze.
Friday *April 16*	A 2.7m piece of fossilized tree, about 260,000,000 years old, has been found at the Six Bells Colliery in south Wales.
Saturday *April 17*	A reported 2755 people are still missing in Mexico after the eruption of El Chinchonal.
Sunday *April 18*	To mark National Samaritan Week, 24 motor cyclists leave Wallbrook, in the City of London, on a 27,350km journey round Britain.
Monday *April 19*	A new Soviet space laboratory, Salyut-7, is launched today. It orbits the earth every 90mins, 274kms out in space.
Tuesday *April 20*	A 45kg wartime bomb is found in mud near the heliport at High Timber Street and Upper Thames Street. The river Thames is closed between Blackfriars and Southwark Bridges.
Wednesday *April 21*	The Queen's birthday. The RSPB has launched a nest-box scheme for Barn Owls, which are declining at an alarming rate.
Thursday *April 22*	The river Thames is getting cleaner! There are at least 101 different species of fish in it now.
Friday *April 23*	St George's Day. Watch out for a Blue Moon as a massive cloud of volcanic debris, over 3km thick, stretches across the Pacific from Mexico to Saudi Arabia, 24km above the earth.

 New Moon

April

The opening month—from the Latin 'aperire' which means to open. Also known as the time of budding.

The Falkland Islands

PEBBLE ISLAND

FOUL BAY

COW BAY
VOLUNTEER BAY
PORT SALVADOR
PORT LOUIS

PORT HOWARD

SAN CARLOS WATER

BERKELEY SOUND

GREEN PATCH

WEST FALKLAND

FALKLAND SOUND

BRENTON LOCH

EAST FALKLAND

FITZROY

STANLEY

DARWIN
GOOSE GREEN

FOX BAY

CHOISEUL SOUND

LAFONIA

NORTH ARM SETTLEMENT

DAILY BEAVER 15p	THE HERALD 12p	DAILY HADDOCK 16p	The Brag 11p
ARGENTINA INVADES THE FALKLAND ISLANDS	'THE EMPIRE STRIKES BACK'— BRITISH TASK FORCE SAILS FOR THE SOUTH ATLANTIC	BRITAIN BLOCKADES THE FALKLANDS	BRITAINS FIRST TEST-TUBE TWINS ARE BORN

Saturday *April 24*	Competitors chosen to run in the second London Marathon receive their start numbers through the post today. West Germany wins the Eurovision Song Contest in Harrogate with 'A Little Bit of Peace'.
Sunday *April 25*	British marines recapture the island of South Georgia in the Falklands in freezing weather, with winds of over 50knots.
Monday *April 26*	The Ministry of Agriculture announces that 40 live Colorado beetles have been found in Italian spinach at Bradford.

> Mount Asama, a 2,499m volcano in central Japan, erupts twice.

Tuesday *April 27*	Twenty-seven live Colorado beetles are found in Spalding, Lincolnshire. Samuel Morse, the inventor of the code, was born in 1791.

> Highest temperature of the month (22°C) is recorded at Linton-on-Ouse in Yorkshire.

Wednesday *April 28*	Skyship 500, the first of a new generation of helium-filled maritime patrol airships, flies over London from Cardington near Bedford.
Thursday *April 29*	Several hundred Chinese weed-eating carp are put into the river Axe at Bleadon today to clear the river and prevent flooding.
Friday *April 30*	Ban on Italian vegetables begins, including spinach, parsley, broccoli, chicory, asparagus, lettuce, onions and aubergines. It will last until June 30th.

The Adventures of a Colorado Beetle

I am a Colorado Potato Beetle.
Some people call me a Potato Bug.
I prefer my proper name.
Long ago my family came from the Rocky Mountains.
They travelled east and crossed the Mississippi in 1864.
In 1874 they reached the east coast of America and the Atlantic.
The next year Germany banned the import of American potatoes.
And in 1876 most of the rest of Europe did the same.
We got across anyway!
By 1922 we had a large colony near Bordeaux in France.
We were very near where all those nice American soldiers had been!
Since then we've done a lot of travelling in Europe.
But I would love to visit Britain.

Hello

Rocky Mountains

POTATOES

AMERICAN POTATOES BANNED!

FRANCE

See you soon

May

Saturday *May 1*	Sir James Barrie's special May Day present to children appeared in Kensington Gardens 70 years ago today: the bronze statue of Peter Pan.
Sunday *May 2*	The Argentine cruiser *General Belgrano* is hit by torpedoes fired from a British submarine at 8pm GMT.
Monday *May 3*	Bank Holiday. Sir David Hunt wins the Mastermind Champion of Champions competition between the 10 people (6 men and 4 women) who have won Mastermind since 1972.
Tuesday *May 4*	The 4100-tonne British destroyer *Sheffield* is hit by an Argentine missile and sinks. The first 3-D pictures seen on British television for 20 years are shown on ITV in the south of England – with the help of green and red spectacles given away with *TV Times!*
Wednesday *May 5*	The oldest quadruplets in the world celebrate their seventieth birthday in Munich.

Children's Day in Japan.

Thursday *May 6*	A 1911 steam locomotive has arrived in Manchester after a month-long journey from Karachi: it's a present from the Pakistan government to the Museum of Science and Industry.
Friday *May 7*	First commercial netting of eels in the river Thames for more than 100 years at Woolwich in east London.
Saturday *May 8*	More than 8,000,000 tulips decorate the floats in the Flower Parade in Spalding, Lincolnshire.

Full Moon

Sunday *May 9*	The 2nd London Marathon: 15,758 people complete the course. Hugh Jones wins in 2hrs 9mins 25secs, and Joyce Smith in 2hrs 29mins and 43secs. The last competitor finished in 6½hrs.
Monday *May 10*	Six small monkeys (pygmy marmosets and moustached tamarin) are discovered in a consignment of wild animals at Gatwick airport.
Tuesday *May 11*	A pillar box near Basingstoke in Hampshire has been closed because a finch is hatching her eggs inside.
Wednesday *May 12*	The new guide at 13th century Thurnham Hall near Lancaster is a 1.8m robot that looks like an Elizabethan Cavalier!
Thursday *May 13*	Two Soviet cosmonauts are launched on a mission to dock with the new Salyut-7 space station.

Friday *May 14*	A pair of Falkland Island pintail ducks arrive at RAF Brize Norton in Oxfordshire from Ascension Island. They were hatched from eggs taken from South Georgia by the British Antarctic Expedition for the *Wildfowl Trust* at Slimbridge, Glos.

Two more Colorado beetles are found—in Italian parsley in Inverness.

Saturday *May 15*	A 7th-century Anglo-Saxon helmet, with hinged sides and a nose guard decorated with copper has been found at Coppergate in York. Crusader, a rare Przewalski's horse, is born at London Zoo.
Sunday *May 16*	The three hundred and twentieth anniversary of the first Punch and Judy show in Covent Garden: Punch reads the lesson in St Paul's Church.
Monday *May 17*	David Scott Cowper, who left Plymouth on September 22 last year, has sailed round the world the wrong way (against the prevailing winds) in his 12.5m yacht *Ocean Bound.* It took him 237 days, smashing the record by 38 days!
Tuesday *May 18*	The first Marmora's Warbler to be seen in Britain is spotted on Midhope Moor in Yorkshire. It is a smokey grey bird, with red rings round the eyes, which usually lives in the Mediterranean.
Wednesday *May 19*	Chelsea Flower Show opens in London. The Queen visits Winchester School, which is celebrating its six hundredth anniversary.
Thursday *May 20*	A golden eagle egg has hatched in the Lake District.
Friday *May 21*	British troops establish a bridgehead at San Carlos on East Falkland, 80kms west of Stanley.
Saturday *May 22*	National Playgroup Week starts today. Princess Diana is now their patron. A black rhino called Esther is born at Regent's Park Zoo in London: she is named after Esther Rantzen.
Sunday *May 23*	Daley Thompson, Britain's Olympic champion, regains his world decathlon record in Austria. His 8707 points beat Guido Kratschmer's 2-year-old record by 58 points. New Moon
Monday *May 24*	A pair of mallard ducks have nested at the M11 motorway police operation control post at Chigwell in Essex.
Tuesday *May 25*	The Orient Express, which has been restored for £1,000,000, makes its maiden trip from Victoria Station to Venice.

May

Takes its name from Maia, the goddess of growth and increase, or from 'maiores', the Latin word for elders, who were honoured this month.

The Anglo Saxons called it 'thrimilce' because cows could be milked three times a day now.

An old Dutch name was 'bloumaand' which means blossoming month.

Papal Tour May 28 – June 2 1982

Pope John Paul II travels over 1600kms by air while he is in Britain and 225kms by road.

Biggest crowds: 350,000 at Coventry
  300,000 at Bellahouston Park, Glasgow
  200,000 at Speke, Liverpool

The Popemobile

There were two different Popemobiles but they both had bullet-proof windows and armour plating. One was a specially adapted Range Rover and the other was a converted 24-tonne, six-wheeled Leyland truck, called a Roadrunner.

London Zoo starts a new Adopt-an-Animal scheme this month. You get an Adoption Certificate, a photograph of the animal you've adopted, a free ticket to the Zoo and your name on a special plaque near the animal.

Here are some of the animals you can adopt, and the price per year:

£10
Spider
Cockroach
Stick Insect
Praying Mantis
Hermit Crab
Ant
Lizard
Gecko
Shrew
Hamster
Dove
Toucan
Cotton Rat
Nile Rat
Carpet Python
Fairy Bluebird

£30
Sugar Glider
Squirrel
Cockatoo
Boa Constrictor
Indian Python
Lovebird
Black Mamba

£60
Lemur
Squirrel Monkey
Marmoset
Porcupine
Sheep

£90
Armadillo
Sooty Mangabey
Wild Boar
Flamingo
Owl
Stork

£500
Chimp
Aardvark

£350
Antelope
Ostrich
Pelican
Giant Anteater
Pig

£750
Cow
Orang-utan
Gorilla
Zebra

£1,000
Leopard
Jaguar

£1,500
Lion
Tiger
Black Rhino
Giraffe

£2,000
Californian Sealion
White Rhino

£5,000
Elephant

£150
Red Panda

Wednesday May 26	Kielder Water in Northumberland is officially opened by the Queen: it is the largest man-made lake in Britain. Aston Villa beat Bayern Munich 1 – 0 in Rotterdam to keep the European Cup in England for the sixth year.
Thursday May 27	The Transglobe Expedition is just over 600km from the North Pole now, drifting slowly south, on an ice floe.
Friday May 28	Pope John Paul II arrives in Britain at the start of a 6-day tour. He lands at Gatwick airport and kisses the tarmac.

 2 Snowy Owls hatch at Regent's Park Zoo in London.

Saturday May 29	The Pope goes to Canterbury Cathedral and then celebrates Mass at Wembley Stadium with 74,000 people.
Sunday May 30	London taxi fares go up: the new minimum fare of 50p covers the first 576m or 2mins 24secs. The rate is then 10p for each 288m or 1min 12secs for 9.6km. After that it is 10p for each 192m or 48secs.
Monday May 31	Bank Holiday. Lightning hits 8 people at Cooper's Hill near Gloucester. They were sheltering under a tree while watching the traditional Bank Holiday cheese rolling races.

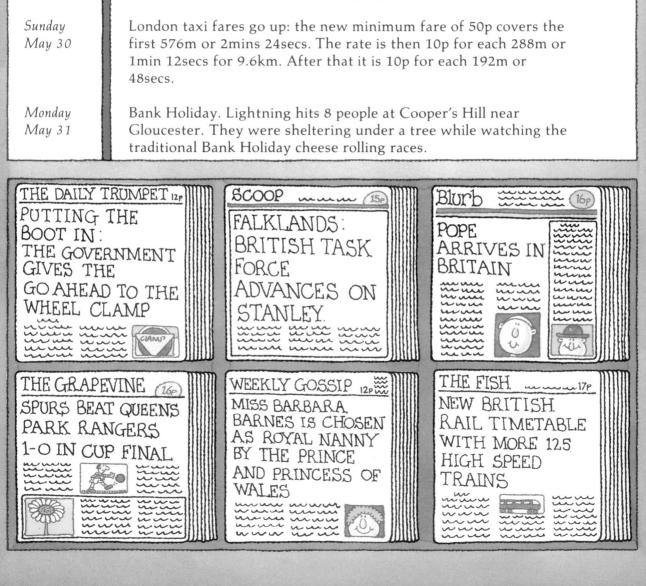

THE DAILY TRUMPET 12p
PUTTING THE BOOT IN: THE GOVERNMENT GIVES THE GO AHEAD TO THE WHEEL CLAMP

SCOOP 15p
FALKLANDS: BRITISH TASK FORCE ADVANCES ON STANLEY.

Blurb 16p
POPE ARRIVES IN BRITAIN

THE GRAPEVINE 16p
SPURS BEAT QUEENS PARK RANGERS 1-0 IN CUP FINAL

WEEKLY GOSSIP 12p
MISS BARBARA BARNES IS CHOSEN AS ROYAL NANNY BY THE PRINCE AND PRINCESS OF WALES

THE FISH 17p
NEW BRITISH RAIL TIMETABLE WITH MORE 125 HIGH SPEED TRAINS

June

Tuesday *June 1*	The Prince of Wales launches the *Pirate Princess*, a £20,000 narrowboat, on the Regent's Canal in London.
Wednesday *June 2*	The Derby at Epsom is won by Golden Fleece, ridden by Pat Eddery, in 2mins 34.21secs. The Pope leaves from Cardiff airport after his 6-day visit.
Thursday *June 3*	Specially adapted Red Indian-style canoes are dropped to Sir Ranulph Fiennes and Charles Burton, of the Transglobe Expedition. They have been stuck on an Arctic ice floe for 6 weeks.
Friday *June 4*	One of the two main anchors from *Ark Royal* is installed in the anchor park at the National Maritime Museum at Greenwich.
Saturday *June 5*	First Rubik's Cube World Championship in Budapest—judged by Erno Rubik.
Sunday *June 6*	London is declared a nuclear free zone by the Greater London Council. An inflatable model of a cruise missile joins 100,000 demonstrators in a CND march to Hyde Park.　Full Moon
Monday *June 7*	President Ronald Reagan and Mrs Nancy Reagan arrive at Heathrow airport at the start of a 2-day visit to Britain.
Tuesday *June 8*	The Queen and President Reagan ride through the Home Park at Windsor Castle — the Queen on Burmese (20) and the President on Centennial (8).
Wednesday *June 9*	The new 20p coin goes into circulation. 300,000,000 have been minted!
Thursday *June 10*	All 10 Common Market countries agree to put the clocks forward by one hour on the last Sunday of March—until 1985!
Friday *June 11*	Delays of up to an hour on the Severn Bridge as engineers begin urgent repair work.
Saturday *June 12*	The Queen's official birthday. British forces capture Argentine positions on the western outskirts of Stanley.
Sunday *June 13*	Bear Day at London Zoo! Free entrance for 5–16-year-olds as long as they bring a bear! Ugly, who is more than a hundred years old, wins the best bear title.
Monday *June 14*	A ceasefire is agreed between British and Argentine forces in the Falklands.

Tuesday *June 15*	Bonnie and Clyde, two polar bears, arrive at Chessington Zoo from West Germany.
Wednesday *June 16*	Times, Tide and Pride, 3 Shire horses, start their 2-week annual holiday on a hop farm in Kent. Swarms of ants in Cwmbran and Pontypool in Wales, after a heat wave.
Thursday *June 17*	No car washing or watering the garden now in Devon or Cornwall! The South West Water Authority says some reservoirs are lower than they were in the drought year of 1976.
Friday *June 18*	A Roman mosaic floor has been unearthed in a vegetable patch at Ilchester in Somerset.
Saturday *June 19*	Schoolchildren in the USA are being asked to contribute 2 cents (just over 1p) each to a £100,000 appeal to repair the Statue of Liberty for its centenary in 1984.
Sunday *June 20*	Russell Byers, from Selby in Yorkshire, scores 1626 points in 3 games, and becomes national Scrabble champion at the grand finals in London.
Monday *June 21*	The Princess of Wales gives birth to a baby boy (3.2kg) at 9.03pm at St Mary's Hospital, Paddington. A good day: there's a new moon and it's the longest day of the year! New Moon
Tuesday *June 22*	Beginning of Ramadan, the Muslim month of fasting from dawn to sunset.
Wednesday *June 23*	Thumper, a wallaby who has been on the hop in Surrey for 10 days, is recaptured by her owner on the Banstead Golf Course, near the sixteenth green!
Thursday *June 24*	Midsummer's Day. A French 'spacionaute' and 2 Soviet cosmonauts are launched from central Asia to join Salyut-7, the orbiting space station. It's the first joint East-West space mission since 1975.
Friday *June 25*	The Girl Guide and Scout Associations receive the Queen Mother's Eightieth Birthday Trophy, the top annual national award of the Keep Britain Tidy Group, in London.
Saturday *June 26*	Two Steppe Eaglets have been bred in captivity at a wild-life rescue centre at Briston in Norfolk, from injured parents.
Sunday *June 27*	Fourth flight of the American space shuttle, on a 7-day mission. Tornado in northern Italy. Heatwave in Sicily.

June

Takes its name from the great goddess Juno, or from 'juniores', the Latin word for young people, who were honoured this month.

The old Dutch name was 'Zomer-maand', which means summer month.

The old Saxon name was 'Sere-monath', which means dry month.

Pollen Count

ANTI POLLEN HELMETS

Grass Pollen is so tiny (about 25,000th of a millimetre in diameter) that you can't see it—or count it very easily! On top of the Nurses' Home at St Mary's Hospital, Paddington in London there is a special machine that sucks in air and traps pollen on a sticky glass slide. Once a day, this slide is removed, put under a microscope and the pollen is counted. Under the magnifying glass, it looks just like tennis balls! There are other pollen-counting machines in different parts of the country.

Grass pollen has no colour or smell.
It doesn't attract bees, butterflies or other pollinators.
It has to be blown by the wind.

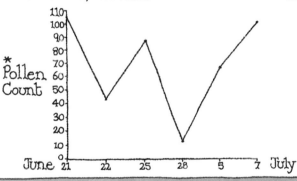

*
Pollen
Count

*According to the Asthma Research Council

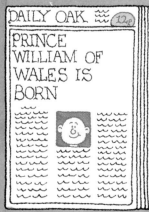

DAILY OAK 12p

PRINCE WILLIAM OF WALES IS BORN

The Town Crier 18p

SPAIN IS HOST TO THE WORLD CUP

NOSEY PARKER 14p

IT'S THE END OF THE FALKLANDS WAR! ARGENTINA SURRENDERS

The Frog 16p

NO TRAINS! BRITISH RAIL ON STRIKE

Monday *June 28*	The Prince and Princess of Wales's son is going to be called William Arthur Philip Louis, and will be known as Prince William of Wales.
Tuesday *June 29*	£50 reward for Cookie, the beer-drinking toucan, who escaped when a gust of wind blew over his cage at Buckland, Gloucestershire. 
Wednesday *June 30*	An extra 'leap' second is added to the last minute of today, to bring the clock into line with solar time.

Five new stamps are issued to mark Maritime England Year.

ADMIRAL BLAKE/TRIUMPH — 19½P

HENRY VIII/MARY ROSE — 15½P

LORD NELSON/HMS VICTORY — 24P

LORD FISHER/HMS DREADNOUGHT — 26P

VISCOUNT CUNNINGHAM/HMS WARSPITE — 29P

NEW 20 PENCE COIN IS ISSUED

Weight: 5gm
Diameter: 21.4mm
Thickness: 1.75mm
Composition: 84% copper,
  16% nickel
Colour: silvery

SHUTTLE ASTRONAUTS DINING IN SPACE

While they're in orbit the three astronauts will eat cream of crab soup, country and green pepper pâté and chocolate mousse (among other things) from plastic tubes!

 Solar time is governed by the rotation of the earth, which is very slightly uneven. So, from time to time, clocks all round the world are stopped for a second to line them up. This is the eleventh adjustment since 1972.

Top Tens of 1982

TOP TEN NAMES 1982*

1. Elizabeth (1)
2. Louise (2)
3. Jane (3)
4. Mary (7)
5. Katherine (8)
6. Sarah (4)
7. Victoria (6)
8. Charlotte (5)
9. Alice (12)
10. Alexandra (9)

1. James (1)
2. Edward (5)
3. William (2)
4. Alexander (3)
5. Thomas (4)
6. John (6)
7. Charles (7)
8. Robert (13)
9. David (8)
10. Richard (11)

*according to *The Times* newspaper

TOP TEN FILMS 1982

(according to *Screen International*)
1. Arthur
2. Chariots of Fire/Gregory's Girl
3. Porky's
4. The Fox and the Hound
5. Condorman
6. Annie
7. Rocky III
8. Herbie Goes Bananas
9. Firefox
10. Who Dares Wins
(N.B. E.T. came out after the figures were compiled!)

TOP TEN SINGLES 1982
(according to *NME*)

1. Eye of the Tiger (Survivor)
2. Come On Eileen (Dexys Midnight Runners)
3. Fame (Irene Carr)
4. The Lion Sleeps Tonight (Tight Fit)
5. Do You Really Want to Hurt Me? (Culture Club)
6. Love Plus One (Haircut 100)
7. Goody Two Shoes (Adam Ant)
8. Golden Brown (The Stranglers)
9. The Land of Make Believe (Bucks Fizz)
10. It Started with a Kiss (Hot Chocolate)

July

Thursday July 1

Happy twenty-first birthday, Princess Diana!
The first new traffic light, which gives bicyclists the right of way, comes into use at Albert Gate in Hyde Park, London.

Friday July 2

Columbia has a close encounter with a piece of space rubbish! The old rocket from a Soviet communications satellite passes within 12.9km of the shuttle above Australia.

Saturday July 3

Martina Navratilova wins the women's singles title at Wimbledon. She beats Chris Evert Lloyd 6–1, 3–6, 6–2. Start of the Tour de France.

Sunday July 4

Independence Day USA. It's the first time that the Wimbledon men's finals are played on Sunday and Jimmy Connors beats John McEnroe 3–6, 6–3, 6–7, 7–6, 6–4

Monday July 5

England goes out of the World Cup, with a goalless draw with Spain.

Tuesday July 6

The first Space Camp has opened at NASA's Marshall Space Flight Centre in Alabama. You can wear a space suit, get a taste of zero gravity and freeze-dried space food!

Wednesday July 7

5000m world record set by David Moorcroft in Oslo: his time is 13mins 0.42secs – 6 secs faster than the previous record, held by Kenya's Henry Rono.

Thursday July 8

Opening by the Queen of the new Chapter House at St Alban's Cathedral.

Friday July 9

Ian Botham makes his highest Test score: 208 runs in 281 minutes! In 3 innings he has scored 403 runs, which beats Sir Leonard Hutton's 399 in 5 innings in 1952.

Saturday July 10

Divers give up their attempt to reach a Spanish galleon, said to be laden with bullion, which sank 400 years ago in Tobermory Bay, off the Isle of Mull.

Sunday July 11

Italy wins the World Cup, beating West Germany 3–1.

Monday July 12

Floods hit the West Country! 113mm of rain falls in 16 hours at Bruton in Somerset, causing floods up to 3m deep.

Tuesday July 13

Cheddar Gorge is closed as a 15-tonne boulder is dislodged. Part crashes through the roof of the cave manager's office, the rest lands in a deserted car park.

Wednesday July 14	A hoard of 74 gold-and-silver coins, the earliest dating from 37BC, are declared treasure trove (i.e. that they belong to the Crown) at Norwich.
Thursday July 15	A special Royal Ale is brewed by Trumans to celebrate the birth of Prince William of Wales. 
Friday July 16	Swans on the river Thames at Abingdon in Oxfordshire are being evacuated because more than a dozen birds have been poisoned.
Saturday July 17	A new 72.9 hectare nature reserve, is opened at Langford Heathfield Common, near Wellington, famous for butterflies in Somerset.

July

 Named in honour of Julius Caesar. The old Dutch name was 'Hooy-maand' hay month, and the old Saxon name was 'Maedd-Monath' because the cattle were turned into the meadow to feed.

1982: YEAR OF THE ECLIPSE!

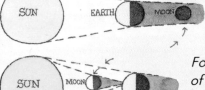

Three total eclipses of the Moon (visible from Britain)

Jan 9   July 6   Dec 30

Four partial eclipses of the Sun (the last one was in 1976)

Jan 25   June 21   July 20   Dec 15

WARNING!   The only safe way to observe an eclipse of the Sun Is to project its image through a hole in a piece of cardboard onto a screen or wall.

July 23:
Four stamps
issued to
celebrate
British
textiles

15½P
British Textiles
William Morris: Strawberry Thief

19½P
British Textiles
Steiner & Co: Untitled

26P
British Textiles
Paul Nash: Cherry Orchard

29P
British Textiles
Andrew Foster: Chevron

Sunday *July 18*	The Queen leaves the King Edward VII Hospital for Officers in London, after having a wisdom tooth out.
Monday *July 19*	An exhibition of treasures recovered from the *Mary Rose* opens today at Longleat in Wiltshire. They range from a dice to a 3-tonne culverin gun dated 1543.
Tuesday *July 20*	Partial eclipse of the sun at about 8pm. Sir Ranulph Fiennes and Charles Burton, of the Transglobe Expedition, have been stranded on an ice floe for 81 days. The floe was originally 4.8km long. It is now less than 1.6km long. New Moon
Wednesday *July 21*	A painting of Pooh Bear by E.H. Shepard fetches £1700 at Sotheby's in London. It is 20 years since the first men landed on the moon.
Thursday *July 22*	Patrick Moore, the astronomer, has had a planet named after him. It is one of tens of thousands of asteroids that lie between the orbits of Mars and Jupiter.
Friday *July 23*	International Whaling Commission, meeting in Brighton, vote for a ban on commercial whaling beginning in 3 years time.
Saturday *July 24*	A small tornado is reported this evening at Eskdalemuir in Scotland.
Sunday *July 25*	Start of the Cutty Sark Tall Ships Race from Falmouth, Cornwall to Lisbon, Portugal and back.
Monday *July 26*	Falklands Islands Service at St Paul's Cathedral, London. Wild mink in the Lake District are becoming a plague.
Tuesday *July 27*	The bridge over the river Orwell at Ipswich is completed. It took 3 years and £24,000,000 to build.
Wednesday *July 28*	Gold bullion half sovereigns, minted in Britain for the first time in 67 years, go on sale today.
Thursday *July 29*	Salyut-6, the 19-tonne Soviet space station, launched in September 1977, re-enters the earth's atmosphere and burns up over the Pacific Ocean.
Friday *July 30*	Two Soviet cosmonauts walk in space for 2hrs 33mins from the orbital space station, Salyut-7, where they have been living for 78 days.
Saturday *July 31*	Children's fares on London Transport buses are now available until 10pm instead of 9pm.

August

Sunday *August 1*	A new letter at the end of car number plates from today – Y instead of X! Ronald MacDonald, from RAF Finningly in Yorkshire, swims the English Channel.
Monday *August 2*	John Hughes and Andrew French win an organized pillow fight at the International Scout Camp at Gilwell Park, Chingford, Essex.
Tuesday *August 3*	An 8-tonne dead whale is blown up by demolition experts on a beach near Southwold in Suffolk.
Wednesday *August 4*	Christening of Prince William of Wales in the Music Room at Buckingham Palace. He wears the Royal Christening Robe, just like King Edward VII, King George VI, the Queen and Prince Charles at their baptisms. Full Moon
Thursday *August 5*	Falklands war widow, Mrs Shirley Sullivan, makes a sponsored parachute jump from over 600m at Aldershot in Hampshire, to raise money for her late husband's battalion.
Friday *August 6*	The world's only airworthy Sunderland flying boat, *Excalibur VIII*, lands on the Thames near Tower Bridge. It goes on show next to *HMS Belfast* to raise money for the South Atlantic Fund.
Saturday *August 7*	Beware the Great Spruce Bark Beetle, which has been found near Ludlow in Shropshire! It is very fond of Christmas trees.
Sunday *August 8*	Donald Muir and Andre Daemen (Canada) break the record for flying round the world in a single-engined aircraft by more than a day. They land in Montreal after flying 38,616km in 6 days 7 hours.
Monday *August 9*	Official opening of Fulham Wave Pool in London. The world submarine cave-diving record is broken in the Bahamas by Martyn Farr, from Gwent: he dives to a depth of 960m in 4½hrs.
Tuesday *August 10*	The row of catalpa trees, which were planted at the foot of Big Ben more than 120 years ago, are dying from pollution.
Wednesday *August 11*	Tonight and tomorrow nights are especially good for the Perseids, one of the best meteor showers of the year.
Thursday *August 12*	Tom McLean (who rowed across the Atlantic in 1969) sails into Falmouth, Cornwall. He left Newfoundland in his tiny boat *Giltspur* (just under 3m long) 50 days 18 hours and 18 minutes ago!
Friday *August 13*	The Berlin Wall is 21 today.

Saturday *August 14*	The RSPB report a record number of osprey breeding in Scotland this year. Twenty seven pairs laid eggs and 46 young have been reared.
Sunday *August 15*	A new hydrofoil between Newhaven and Dieppe is launched.
Monday *August 16*	The Falklands celebrate the Princess of Wales's twenty-first birthday, a bit late, with a special stamp issue.
Tuesday *August 17*	Rebel, Britain's oldest working police dog, retires in Stroud, Gloucestershire. Happy tenth birthday to *Jesus Christ Superstar*, Britain's longest-running musical!
Wednesday *August 18*	Australian Dick Smith lands at Stornoway in the Hebrides and becomes the first man to fly single-handed across the Atlantic in a helicopter.
Thursday *August 19*	Svetlana Savitskaya (34) becomes the second Soviet spacewoman when she is launched in a Soyuz spacecraft on a mission to the Salyut-7 space station. New Moon
Friday *August 20*	Ice-patrol ship *HMS Endurance* sails into Chatham harbour after more than 10 months in the Antarctic.
Saturday *August 21*	King Sobhuza of Swaziland, the world's longest-reigning monarch, dies at the age of 83. He ruled for 61 years, had 100 wives and about 600 children.
Sunday *August 22*	A giant game of chess, with people as pieces, is played at Portmeirion, Gwynedd. Two hundred years of cricket at Groombridge in Sussex is celebrated by a game in 18th century dress between a local team and one from Tunbridge Wells.
Monday *August 23*	Peter Bird, from London, sets out from San Francisco to row single-handed non-stop across the Pacific from USA to Australia.
Tuesday *August 24*	The Great Spruce Bark Beetle is moving west. It has been spotted in South Wales.
Wednesday *August 25*	On this day in 1875, Captain Matthew Webb became the first person to swim the English Channel: it took him 21hrs 45mins from Dover to Calais.
Thursday *August 26*	The £7,000,000 crane barge *Tog Mor* (Big Lifter) is ready in the Solent to lift the wreck of the Tudor flagship, the *Mary Rose*. It has a helicopter pad and an accommodation deck for 90 men.

August

Named in honour of the Roman Emperor Augustus, whose lucky month it was.
The old Dutch name was 'Oost-maand' – harvest month.
The old Saxon name was 'Weodmonath' – weed month.

The Transglobe Expedition

Sir Ranulph Fiennes and Charles Burton reached the South Pole on December 17, 1980. They went on to New Zealand and Australia and then sailed to Los Angeles and Vancouver in Canada. After a boat trip down the Yukon river, they went through the North West Passage to Ellesmere Island, where they set up their winter base camp at Alert. After 4 months there, preparing equipment and training in permanent darkness, they set off to cross the Arctic for the North Pole on February 13, 1982. They travelled on skidoos, which are a bit like snow motor bikes, with a single short ski at the front—each towing about 272kg of fuel and equipment. With them went Bothie, a Jack Russell terrier, who became the first dog to visit both North and South Poles! They reached the North Pole at 11.30pm GMT, on April 10. On August 4 they were picked up by their support ship the *Benjamin Bowring*, and arrived back in Greenwich on August 29, having circumnavigated the globe via both the North and South Poles.

THE ROUTE OF THE BRITISH TRANSGLOBE EXPEDITION 1980-1982.

DAILY OWL 17p
PLAGUE OF SUPER-HAMSTERS IN BURNT OAK, LONDON

Eye Spy 12p
AMERICAN ASHBY-HARPER (65) IS THE OLDEST PERSON TO SWIM THE ENGLISH CHANNEL

FRED'S NEWSPAPER 15p
FOREST FIRES IN THE SOUTH OF FRANCE

THE GALAXY 14p
STRIKE BY CARTOONISTS AT WALT-DISNEY

Friday *August 27*	Operation Apple Pie at Orpington, Kent: the world's biggest apple pie is made from 12,894kg of apples, 2876.5kg of flour and 2210kg of sugar. It measures 12m by 7m and weighs 12.5 tonnes!
Saturday *August 28*	Bill Dunlop, who is sailing across the Atlantic from west to east in *Wind's Will* (2.8m long), has run out of food and is living on water.
Sunday *August 29*	The Transglobe Expedition arrives home at Greenwich, after 3 years and 56,327km, aboard their support ship, the *Benjamin Bowring*. Bill Dunlop sails into Falmouth in Cornwall, after 78 days at sea, taking the record for the smallest craft to cross the Atlantic from west to east from Tom McLean (see August 12).
Monday *August 30*	Bank Holiday. First Custard-Pie Throwing Championships at Farnborough in Hampshire. The 500-year-old Major Oak, where Robin Hood hid in Sherwood Forest, is badly damaged by fire.
Tuesday *August 31*	The biggest strawstack in the world is built at Birdlip in Gloucestershire. It is 45.7m long, 9.1m high and made of 40,000 bales of straw!

1982 Anniversaries

800th anniversary of the birth of St Francis of Assisi

350th anniversary of the birth of Sir Christopher Wren

250th anniversary of the Royal Opera House, Covent Garden

100th anniversary of the British Veterinary Association

75th anniversary of the Scout Movement

50th anniversary of the Monte Carlo Rally

40th anniversary of 'Desert Island Discs'

30th anniversary of the Queen's accession to the throne

September

Wednesday *September 1*	Whooping cough epidemic. 1941 new cases were reported last week, bringing the total this year to over 33,000.
Thursday *September 2*	The Department of Transport announces that drivers and front seat passengers will have to wear seat belts from January 31, 1983.
Friday *September 3*	The £870,000 Blackpool illuminations are switched on by the commander of the South Atlantic Task Force, Rear-Admiral John Woodward. It is their fiftieth year. Full Moon
Saturday *September 4*	Motorised police hang gliders on patrol in Los Angeles! They have bullet-proof seats and spotlights for night flying.
Sunday *September 5*	John Berry (21) is bitten by a baby adder and gives up his attempt to live for 70 days in a tank of poisonous snakes at Rhyl. It is his thirty-eighth day!

> Storms and flooding in Sussex
> 80 mm of rain at Southreps in Norfolk

Monday *September 6*	Sir Ranulph and Lady Fiennes visit Bothie, their Jack Russell terrier, who is in quarantine after his trip to the Poles.
Tuesday *September 7*	Karen Austin (18) becomes the first girl to win the title 'Young Chef of the Year' with hot sweet chocolate-and-orange souffles.
Wednesday *September 8*	Daley Thompson wins a gold medal for the decathlon and sets a world record at the European athletics championships in Athens. He scores 8744 points.
Thursday *September 9*	A toy train, made at the beginning of the century, is sold for £4200 at Christie's in South Kensington, London.
Friday *September 10*	Jacqui Hampson (13) from Weymouth becomes the youngest girl to swim the English Channel: it took her 16hrs to cross from Folkestone to Calais.
Saturday *September 11*	Thamesday on the river between Westminster and Hungerford bridges, in London. Steve Cram wins a gold medal in Athens: he runs the 1500m in 3mins 36.49secs.
Sunday *September 12*	Anthony Andrews, who played Sebastian Flyte in 'Brideshead Revisited' is voted 1982's Best Dressed Man.

> Severe gales in northern Scotland

Monday *September 13*	Southampton's 14th International Boat Show opens at Mayflower Park.

Tuesday *September 14*	The wreck of Britain's first submarine, *Holland I*, which is being lifted from the seabed off Plymouth, is in such good condition that a china lavatory with a wooden seat has been found intact!
Wednesday *September 15*	*HMS Belfast* is towed downstream to Tilbury dry dock to be be overhauled and have her bottom scraped.
Thursday *September 16*	New 12-week-old puppies ('W' Litter) are presented to their handlers at the Metropolitan Police Dog Training Establishment near Bromley in Kent. Their names are Warspite, Wizzard, Winter, Witch, Whisper and Weedell.
Friday *September 17*	The 16,000 tonne *HMS Invincible* returns to Portsmouth from the Falklands. A poisonous Mexican red-kneed tarantula spider, 3 parakeets and a pair of cockateels are stolen from a pet shop in Islington, London. New Moon
Saturday *September 18*	Rosh Hashanah, the first day of the Jewish New Year. The apple crop in Kent and Sussex is the best for 20 years!
Sunday *September 19*	Twelve wolves escape from the Cardigan Wildlife Park at Llechryd in Wales.
Monday *September 20*	American runner Stan Cottrell (39) sets off from Edinburgh on a 5149km marathon across Europe. He hopes to reach Gibraltar on December 8.
Tuesday *September 21*	Prince William of Wales, aged 3 months, has his inoculation against whooping cough at Balmoral.
Wednesday *September 22*	Beautiful sunsets in some parts of the country are probably caused by the volcano at El Chinchonal in Mexico. The huge clouds of dust and gases that were released into the atmosphere play tricks with the light!
Thursday *September 23*	Cub Scout Matthew Steadman (9), the 2nd Llandudno pack, is the individual winner of the National Cub Scout Tea-making Competition. Autumn equinox
Friday *September 24*	A Government-sponsored survey reveals that Enid Blyton books and *Beano* comic are favourite reading among 11-year-olds!
Saturday *September 25*	Watch out for wizards, giants, ogres, skeletons, hobgoblins, halflings, and underhulks! About 500 miniatures are used in a Dungeons and Dragons demonstration at Games Day at the Royal Horticultural Hall, London. *Sunday Times* Fun Run in Hyde Park, London.

September

This was the seventh month when the year used to start in March.
The old Dutch name was 'Herst-maand' – autumn month and the old Saxon name was 'Gerst-monath' – barley month.

Year of the Butterfly — a Bulletin

Britain's butterfly population is declining because of the loss of natural habitats.

Woods and coppices are being replaced by high (often coniferous) forests.

Over 225,307km of hedgerows and verges have disappeared since 1945.

Marshes and heathland are being reclaimed.

Some endangered species

Grave Concern
Heath Fritillary
Silver-spotted Skipper
Swallowtail
Adonis Blue
Large Tortoiseshell

Concern
Chequered Skipper
White-letter Hairstreak
Black Hairstreak
High Brown Fritillary
Glanville Fritillary
Marsh Fritillary

September 8 Two new stamps are issued to celebrate Information Technology Year.
15 ½ pence Development of Communications
26 pence Modern Technological Aids

THE DAILY PEEP 16p

DUTCH SOLDIERS ARE ALLOWED TO WEAR EARRINGS WITH THEIR UNIFORMS

THE REPORTER

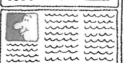
COMMONWEALTH GAMES OPEN IN BRISBANE, AUSTRALIA

NO.1 15p

SUSAN BATTEN IS BRITAINS FIRST FULL-TIME FIREWOMAN

DAILY SPOTLIGHT

WAR IN BEIRUT CONTINUES BASHIR GAMAYEL IS KILLED

Sunday *September 26*	A freak whirlwind damages homes in north Belfast.
Monday *September 27*	Gales and heavy rain: flood water sweeps away tropical fish and man-eating piranhas from an aquarium in the Isle of Man. Drought in Australia is driving kangaroos and wombats out of the bush to look for food in Melbourne.
Tuesday *September 28*	During a lull in high winds, the 125-tonne lifting cradle is positioned alongside the wreck of the *Mary Rose* on the bed of the Solent.
Wednesday *September 29*	Only 12 days to go to the World Conker Championships at Ashton near Oundle in Northamptonshire, and there's not a conker to be found there! The organisers are collecting 3000 from other places.
Thursday *September 30*	The Duke of Edinburgh opens the Commonwealth Games in Brisbane, Australia. Matilda, a 12m tall, tractor-driven kangaroo (the games' mascot) arrives with 12 children in her pouch!

Champions of 1982

Rose of the Year	Mountbatten
Newspaper of the Year	*Daily Mirror*
Museum of the Year	City Museum and Art Gallery, Stoke-on-Trent
Miss Pears	Elena Lartey
Champion Show Jumper	St James (Nick Skelton)
Supreme Cattle Champion	High Voltage
Pet of the Year	Bothie
Editor of the Year	Harold Evans (*The Times*)
Best Racing Pigeon	Casa Mia Prince
Pipeman of the Year	Dave Lee Travis
Miss World	Miss Dominican Republic
Teapot Award	Claris Tea Room, Biddenden, Kent
Time Magazine Award of the Year	The Computer (for the first time it is not a man or a woman!)
Superkid '82	Ky Ho
Shepherd of the Year	George Reid
Best-dressed man	Anthony Andrews
BBC Sports Personality	Daley Thompson
Sportswoman of the Year	Wendy Norman
Car of the Year	Ford Sierra
Supreme Champion at Crufts	Grayco Hazelnut
Toy of the Year	Star Wars Toys

October

Friday *October 1*	The last telegrams ever are sent at 11.59pm – from now on it's tele-messages! The mini Thames Flood Barrier is opened at Barking Creek in Essex.
Saturday *October 2*	Exhibition of 120 teddy bears opens at the Museum of Lincolnshire Life—including Mrs Thatcher's Humphrey!
Sunday *October 3*	The Black Dyke Mills Band wins the European Brass Band Championship. Full Moon
Monday *October 3*	A runaway porcupine is captured after a chase at Carshalton in Surrey.
Tuesday *October 5*	Neroli Fairhall, from New Zealand, who is confined to a wheelchair, wins a gold medal for archery at the Commonwealth Games.
Wednesday *October 6*	Venice floods: the water reaches 1.3m above sea level.
Thursday *October 7*	Photo-finish in the 200m at the Commonwealth Games: after 20 minutes, the judges declare that it is a dead heat between Alan Wells (Scotland) and Mike McFarlane (England)!
Friday *October 8*	A new air exclusion zone in the Falklands allows penguins to hatch their young in peace.
Saturday *October 9*	A team of RAF athletes run 241km from Athens to Sparta in Greece, retracing the famous run by Pheidippides in 490 BC when he went to get help against the Persians.
Sunday *October 10*	Soviet cosmonauts Anatoly Berezovoy and Valentine Lebedev have been in space for more than 150 days now, aboard Salyut-7 space station.
Monday *October 11*	*Mary Rose*, Henry VIII's flagship, which sank in the Solent in 1545, is lifted from the sea bed.
Tuesday *October 12*	'Salute to the Task Force' celebrations in London: 1250 Falklands veterans parade through the City.
Wednesday *October 13*	Four new stamps are issued by the Post Office in honour of the British Motor Industry.
Thursday *October 14*	About 750 people are evacuated at Cliff Quay in Ipswich because of clouds of toxic smoke from a fertilizer warehouse that caught fire.

Friday *October 15*	Ted Toleman, from Essex, breaks his own world off-shore powerboat speed record on Lake Windermere with an average speed of 176.9kph.
Saturday *October 16*	Two astronomers at the Mount Palomar Observatory in California, see Halley's Comet between Saturn and Uranus, heading for the Sun.
Sunday *October 17*	A 20-tonne humpback whale is washed up on the beach at Gileston, South Glamorgan – the first of the species to be found in Britain since records began in 1913.

New moon

Five earthquakes in central Italy (the strongest measures 4.4 on the Richter Scale).

Monday *October 18*	Official opening of a special cattle grid on the A4117 over Clee Hill near Ludlow, Shropshire. It is the first to be fitted with an escape ramp for hedgehogs.
Tuesday *October 19*	Launch of Radio Gosh, the new service for the Hospital for Sick Children in Great Ormond Street, London.
Wednesday *October 20*	Thousands of people are evacuated from their homes after a dam bursts near Valencia in Spain.
Thursday *October 21*	American millionaire, Malcolm Forbes, flies over Beijing, China in a hot-air balloon.
Friday *October 22*	The 1982 Motor Show opens at the National Exhibition Centre near Birmingham.
Saturday *October 23*	The EPCOT Centre at Disney World in Florida is opened. It stands for Experimental Prototype Community of Tomorrow!
Sunday *October 24*	More than 16,000 runners take part in the New York Marathon. Alberto Salazar, from Oregon, wins it for the third time running in 2hrs 9mins 48secs. British Summer Time ends at 2am GMT. Clocks go back an hour!
Monday *October 25*	Dr Who (alias Peter Davison) meets the winners of the Post Office's Letter Writing Competition: Timothy Conway (12), Timothy Milward (8), Jacqueline Hancock (16) and David Harrop (12). The theme was a letter to someone from another planet.
Tuesday *October 26*	Bo-Bo, a king cormorant from the Falklands, who crashed on *HMS Bristol* and broke a wing, is out of quarantine at London Zoo.
Wednesday *October 27*	John Sanders is sighted off west Australia: he is circumnavigating the globe twice in his 10m sloop *Perie Banou*.

October

From the Latin word 'octo' which means eight: it used to be the eighth month in the old Roman calendar.
'Wyn-maand' in old Dutch means wine month!
'Winter-fylleth' in Old English, which means winter full moon.

Beaver Scouts, for 6–8-year-old boys, starts this month. They wear turquoise scarves with maroon toggles and meet in colonies of between 12 and 18—usually once a week. Their motto is FUN AND FRIENDS!

TOP TEN MEDAL WINNERS AT THE COMMONWEALTH GAMES

	Gold	Silver	Bronze	Total
Australia	39	39	29	107
England	38	38	32	108
Canada	26	23	33	82
Scotland	8	6	12	26
New Zealand	5	8	13	26
India	5	8	3	16
Nigeria	5	0	8	13
Kenya	4	2	4	10
Wales	4	4	1	9
Bahamas	2	2	2	6

The *Mary Rose*

The 7000-tonne *Mary Rose* was one of the flagships of the English fleet which sailed from Portsmouth on July 19, 1545 to meet the French. The other was the *Great Harry*, 1000 tonnes. Only 1.5km out, the *Mary Rose* suddenly foundered and sank, watched by King Henry VIII and his court from Southsea Castle. There were 715 men on board, including Vice-Admiral Sir George Carew: 35, at the most, survived. So far the bones of 120 men have been recovered from the ship.

Thursday *October 28*	Five Bewick Swans arrive back from Arctic Russia at the Wildfowl Trust at Slimbridge in Gloucestershire – a week later than last year. Cocky, the sulphur-crested cockatoo, who lived at London Zoo since 1925, dies. International Hallo Day
Friday *October 29*	More than 20 whales are discovered stranded on a sandbank off the mouth of the river Haven, near Boston in Lincolnshire. They are between 4.5m and 7.6m long. 
Saturday *October 30*	Between 40 and 50 whales are stranded on Bank Buoy Sands now. A huge rescue operation is mounted to coax them out to sea.
Sunday *October 31*	Hallowe'en! John Sanders sails into Perth harbour in West Australia, after a double circumnavigation of the globe that took 420 days.

Goodbye Cocky!

Cocky was given to Regent's Park Zoo in London in 1925 by a family who had owned him since the beginning of the century. At the zoo he greeted everyone with a piercing screech and a loud HALLO! In 1980 he was awarded a certificate and medal by the Burlington Arcade Society for making London a friendlier place. The medal was inscribed with the words YOUR GOOD MANNERS HELPED LONDON, COCKY.

October 8 : Four new stamps to honour the British Motor Industry

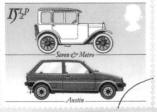
15½P — Seven & Metro — Austin

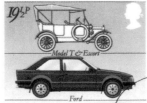
19½P — Model T & Escort — Ford

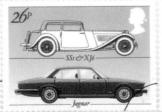
26P — SS1 & XJ6 — Jaguar

29P — Silver Ghost & Silver Spirit — Rolls-Royce

DAILY SQUIGGLE 16P
TWO VC'S AWARDED IN FALKLANDS WAR – 835 OTHER AWARDS

THE SCROLL 18P
POLAND BANS THE TRADES UNION SOLIDARITY

NEWSREEL 16P
PANIC AS NY STOCK EXCHANGE SUFFERS BIGGEST ONE-DAY FALL SINCE 1929

DAILY KNIB 20P
MARY ROSE RISES FROM ITS WATERY GRAVE

November

Monday *November 1*	A school of 16 pilot whales is washed up at Holbeach in Lincolnshire. Full Moon
Tuesday *November 2*	Introducing Superted, who appears (in Welsh) on the first day of Wales's new fourth television channel S4C. A word quiz 'Countdown' and the first edition of 'Brookside' kick off Channel 4 in England.
Wednesday *November 3*	The State Opening of Parliament. 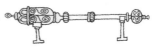
Thursday *November 4*	Richard Noble tries to break the world land-speed record in his jet-powered car *Thrust II* in the Black Rock Desert, Nevada. He averages 949.3kph over 2 runs but is 51.4kph short of the 12-year-old record held by the American Gary Gabelich.
Friday *November 5*	A new exhibition about gorillas opens at the Natural History Museum in London, including Guy the Gorilla who has been preserved and stuffed by the museum's taxidermy department.
Saturday *November 6*	Fourteenth London Championship of small livestock at the Harrow Leisure Centre.
Sunday *November 7*	London is safe from flooding! The first public demonstration of the new Thames Flood Barrier at Woolwich.
Monday *November 8*	Beginning of Poppy Week! Royal Variety Performance at the Theatre Royal, Drury Lane.
Tuesday *November 9*	Lancelot, the 22-year-old Bewick Swan, is back for his 20th winter at Slimbridge Wildfowl Trust in Gloucestershire. He has flown 4183kms from Russia, with his third mate, Elaine, and his latest offspring, Excalibur.
Wednesday *November 10*	A bronze statue of Guy the Gorilla, who died in 1978, aged 32, is unveiled at London Zoo.
Thursday *November 11*	American space shuttle Columbia is launched (sixty-eight thousandths of a second late) on its fifth flight from Cape Canaveral, Florida, at 12.19 GMT. It carries a crew of 4 and 2 commercial communications satellites.
Friday *November 12*	A cat called Sedgewick blacks out half the lights in Cambridge. He strayed into an electricity sub-station and shorted the power lines.
Saturday *November 13*	Lord Mayor's Show in London: the parade of 24 carriages and 63 floats leaves Guildhall at 11am. Firework display on the river Thames at 5pm.

Sunday *November 14*	First heavy snow of the winter in Scotland and Derbyshire. Two main roads (the A54 and the A53) are closed for 4hrs. Hailstorms in Sussex!
Monday *November 15*	Eight members of the Red Devils parachute team, each with a bottle of Beaujolais Nouveau strapped to his body, splash down from an Army helicopter in the river Thames. One bottle comes adrift and lands in Covent Garden.  New Moon
Tuesday *November 16*	Columbia lands safely at Edwards Air Force Base in California.
Wednesday *November 17*	A Pomarine skua, from arctic Russia, is spotted on the North Lake at Willen, Milton Keynes.
Thursday *November 18*	Prince Andrew switches on an avenue of Christmas trees lit by 55,000 bulbs in Regent Street, London. Miss Dominican Republic (Mariasela Alvarez) becomes Miss World 1982.
Friday *November 19*	The 1982 Asian Games open in Delhi, India in front of a crowd of 75,000. Nearly 5000 athletes from 33 countries take part.
Saturday *November 20*	Feminists object to signs like this in bicycle lanes in Oxford.
Sunday *November 21*	A fish bone lodges in the throat of Queen Elizabeth, the Queen Mother at dinner. She has it removed at the King Edward VII Hospital for Officers in London.
Monday *November 22*	A flying gecko, born at London Zoo on August 23, goes missing.
Tuesday *November 23*	Professor Francis Graham Smith is appointed Astronomer Royal. He succeeds Sir Martin Ryle. Shortage of mistletoe at the sales in Tenbury Wells, on the borders of Herefordshire and Worcestershire.
Wednesday *November 24*	Operation Sky Quest is unveiled at the Royal Aeronautical Society in London: next year a hot-air balloon, more than 55m tall, will challenge the record flight of 16,764m.
Thursday *November 25*	Barnado's Champion Children of the Year lunch at the Savoy Hotel in London. Vietnamese refugee, Ky Ho, is named Superkid '82.
Friday *November 26*	A fly-past and a 21-gun salute marks the official opening of the £1,400,000 Henry Moore art gallery and sculpture centre in Leeds by the Queen.

Saturday *November 27*	Free trees for gardens in Oldham! The council plans to plant 1,000,000 in the next 5 years. Casa Mia Prince, a three-year-old cock, is judged best racing pigeon at the Old Comrades Show in London.
Sunday *November 28*	Two climbers, trapped by blizzards near the summit of Mount Cook (3777.7m) in New Zealand, are rescued by helicopter.
Monday *November 29*	The Victorian West Pier at Brighton is given the highest grade in the classification of listed buildings.
Tuesday *November 30*	St Andrew's Day. Menus in Braille are being introduced at restaurants at Heathrow airport, London.

HAMBURGER AND CHIPS

November

Takes its name from the Latin word for nine, 'novem', because it used to be the ninth month in the old Roman calendar, when the year began in March. The old Saxon name was 'Wind-monath'—wind month. The old Dutch name was 'Slaght- maand'—slaughter month.

The Thames Barrier

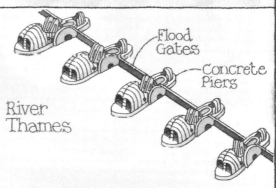

Flood Gates

Concrete Piers

River Thames

The Thames Barrier is the world's largest movable flood barrier, took 8 years to build and cost £435 million. It is made up of a series of gates that stretch end to end across the river at Woolwich. When they are not in use, they rest on concrete sills on the river bed but, when needed, swing up through 90° between their concrete piers to form a continuous steel wall 520m long. This seals off the upper Thames and London from the sea. The 4 main openings each have a clear span of 61m, and the 4 main gates are over 20 metres high and each weigh about 3,700 tonnes. The gates are controlled and powered from the southern shore and only take 30mins to close.

High tide levels in central London are rising by about 75cm a century!

Central London was last flooded in 1928: 14 people drowned.

December

Wednesday *December 1*	A new Royal Navy submarine, the 4500-tonne *Turbulent*, is launched at Barrow-in Furness. Full Moon
Thursday *December 2*	The Princess of Wales visits the Hospital for Sick Children, Great Ormond Street, London.
Friday *December 3*	Tommy Steele unveils his statue of Elinor Rigby in Stanley Street, Liverpool. During casting, he put in a 4-leaf clover, football socks and comics—among other things!
Saturday *December 4*	The Law Courts in the Strand are 100 years old today.
Sunday *December 5*	Christmas trees cost between £1 and £1.50 per 30.5cm this year!
Monday *December 6*	The lighthouse on Skule Skerry, 51.5km west of Orkney in the Atlantic, goes automatic. It is Britain's remotest lighthouse and has been manned for 88 years by 3 keepers.
Tuesday *December 7*	High Voltage, a cross-bred Charolais-Aberdeen Angus steer, wins the Supreme Cattle Championship at Smithfield in London.
Wednesday *December 8*	Prince Edward flies to Scott Base in Antarctica, to visit the South Pole.
Thursday *December 9*	The lights on the Christmas tree in Trafalgar Square in London (a present from the people of Oslo) are switched on at 6pm by the Norwegian Ambassador.
Friday *December 10*	The Soviet cosmonauts Anatoly Berezovoy and Valentin Lebedev return to earth after a record-breaking 211 days on board the Salyut-7 space station. The previous space endurance record was 185 days.
Saturday *December 11*	National Cat Club Show with about 2000 cats, including Blue Peter's Jack and Jill, at Olympia in London.
Sunday *December 12*	About 30,000 women hold hands and form a human chain around the 14.5km perimeter fence of the American air base at Greenham Common in Berkshire.
Monday *December 13*	Twelve children from Holland Park School in London go to No. 10 Downing Street to interview Mrs Thatcher for Thames Television's programme CBTV.
Tuesday *December 14*	Best night for Geminid meteor shower! Father Christmas gives a party at 11 Downing Street.

Wednesday *December 15*	Partial eclipse of the Sun, visible from Britain between 7.22am and 11.41am. Queen Elizabeth, the Queen Mother, presents the Children of Courage Awards at Westminster Abbey.
Thursday *December 16*	George Reid, from Dunkeld in Perthshire, becomes Shepherd of the Year.
Friday *December 17*	A small green plaque between Henry James, T.S. Eliot and Lord Byron is dedicated to Lewis Carroll in Poets' Corner, Westminster Abbey.
Saturday *December 18*	Father Christmas reads a story on (01) 246 8080!
Sunday *December 19*	Hans Tholstrup sets off from Perth in Australia to drive over 4000km to Sydney in a solar-powered car. New film categories come into force. The old categories were 'U', 'A', 'AA' and 'X'!
Monday *December 20*	The BBC's Richard Baker interviews Peter Pan and Wendy 6m above the stage at the Barbican in London. He is supported by 2 wires, rather than the usual 1!
Tuesday *December 21*	Father Christmas parachutes out of a plane 762m above Waterville, Maine, in America. He lands in a ploughed field.
Wednesday *December 22*	Prince William, aged 6 months, meets press photographers for the first time wearing a white silk romper suit. Shortest day of the year.
Thursday *December 23*	Two students are rescued in the Cairngorms after spending 12 hours in a snow hole.
Friday *December 24*	Special cheap telephone rates over Christmas and the New Year: a 3-minute call to Australia or New Zealand costs £2.48, including VAT. Could it be anything to do with *E.T.*?
Saturday *December 25*	The first day since December 4 without snow falling somewhere in the U.K. A very White Christmas in USA, where there are blizzard conditions. More than 2000 people are stranded at Denver Airport.
Sunday *December 26*	Traditional Boxing Day swims along the Sussex coast – at Eastbourne, Hastings, Worthing, Brighton and Bexhill.
Monday *December 27*	Shaun Carter, an ambulance driver from Eastbourne, has camped outside the main entrance of Selfridge's in Oxford Street, London, for nearly 2 weeks and has raised almost £9,000 for leukaemia research.

Tuesday *December 28*	An omelette that weighs more than 558kg has been made in Bad Lauterberg in West Germany. 6000 eggs were used, nearly 30kg of fat, 45kg of bacon and 25kg of onions!
Wednesday *December 29*	Two-week amnesty on library fines in Wiltshire! A book taken out in 1967 has been returned to a Chippenham mobile library.
Thursday *December 30*	Total eclipse of the moon, but it's not visible from Britain!
Friday *December 31*	The New Year's Honours List: 677 people are honoured. Full Moon

December

10

Takes its name from the Latin word for ten, 'decem': it used to be the tenth month in the old Roman calendar.

10

Faces of the Year

Bothie
Feb 13

Columbia
March 22,
June 27, Nov 11

Eagle
March 27

El Chinchonal
March 29

The Task Force
April 5

Salyut-7
April 19

The Colorado
Beetle
April 26

The Pope
May 28

The 20 pence piece
June 9

Prince William
June 21

Daley Thompson
Sept 8

Neroli Fairhall
Oct 5

The *Mary Rose*
Oct 11

The EPCOT Centre
Oct 23

Cocky
Oct 28

Superted
Nov 2

Guy the Gorilla
Nov 5, Nov 10

The Thames Barrier
Nov 7

Lancelot
Nov 9

E.T.
Dec 10

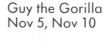

'IN' in 1982

Deely-boppers (antennae)
Aerobics
Leg warmers
Electronic games
Role-playing games
Break dancing
E.T.